D1537240

COPS & GOD

THE JOURNAL

"I AM WITH YOU ALWAYS"

BY POLICE SERGEANT STEVEN L ROGERS

PUBLISHED BY
ROGERS GROUP INC
P.O. BOX 225
NUTLEY N.J. 07110

Copyright 1998
Rogers Group Incorporated

ISBN: 1-57502-726-7

Printed in the USA by

MORRIS PUBLISHING

3212 East Highway 30 • Kearney, NE 68847 • 1-800-650-7888

THE TWELVE STORIES WRITTEN IN THIS BOOK ARE DEDICATED
TO THE TWELVE APOSTLES WHO CARRIED THE LIGHT OF
CHRIST DURING THE DARKEST DAYS OF EARLY BIBLICAL TIMES
SO THAT WE MAY RECEIVE THE LIGHT OF CHRIST TODAY.

In Memory of:

PETER

ANDREW

JAMES

JOHN

PHILIP

BARTHOLOMEW

MATTHEW

THOMAS

JAMES

THADDDAEUS

SIMON

MATTHIAS

THIS JOURNAL IS DEDICATED TO MY WIFE EVELYN WHO PLANTED THE SPIRITUAL SEED TO COMPLETE THIS WORK TO MY MOTHER ANN, MY FATHER BUDDY, MY SON STEVEN, MY DAUGHTERS KRYSTAL, SHANNON, AND STEPHANIE.

INTRODUCTION

Since writing my first book, *Cops & God "A Loyal Partnership"* and my second book, TEARS, *"From A Fathers Eyes"* I have been wanting to write a journal which shares the commitment Jesus Christ has to people who demonstrate their devotion, love, and obedience toward *him; Cops & God, "I Am With You Always"* is that journal.

Throughout my career as a police officer I have witnessed the good, the bad, and the ugly sides of mankind. I have seen heroic people risk their lives to save a fellow human being or a helpless animal in trouble. And I have seen people take lives, destroy property, and terrorize the weak and helpless.

Most of what I have witnessed in the past and continue to witness today are a vast number of men, women, and young adults striving to achieve goals which were not imagined years ago by a generation which lived through four major wars and a depression.

These goal oriented people are from all walks of life. The one thing they all have in common is that they are relatively successful in what they do. Their desire to succeed and be the best in their chosen profession becomes their driving force.

In one sense it is good to be goal oriented and to use the mind and the imagination to reach goals and ultimately succeed in every endeavor It is good to dream and to see those dreams come true by working diligently But in another sense it is not good when we use only our mind and imagination and not our heart and spirit in our quest to reach the goals we set and to see our dreams come true.

I have no doubt that you, the reader of this book, has at one time in your life journeyed into one of life's raging storms. And no doubt you have read numerous books and tried various methods to calm that storm, be it caused by family problems, medical woes, financial worries, or other matters in your life which seemed too insurmountable for you to overcome.

Thankfully, most of us overcome the problems we face. But sadly to say, most of the solutions many people apply to problem-solving are temporary in the sense that they simply delay the inevitable which eventually leads to bigger problems.

Problems and difficulties will always be a part of life But the question all of us must ask at one point in time is; "Has anything I have tried in my quest to solve my problems given me the peace I seek and the healing I need when my heart is broken and spirit wounded?"

Many people suffering from the ills of this world consume their time by reading "healing" books; by using computer technology; by listening and viewing audio and video tapes; and by trying every other man made quick fix-it scheme invented to solve problems and find peace. The result is failure! They used the mind and imagination without the heart and the spirit

Through all the sounds of turning pages, modems, faxes, computers, and every other kind of electronic problem-solving gadget we have invented, most people have ignored the simple instructional guide about life which is available to every man, woman, and child And in ignoring this guide they have allowed the sun to set on

II

its famous author whose advice and words of wisdom have helped mankind since the day God created the heavens and the earth The guide is known as the Bible. Its author is Jesus Christ.

Since the day Adam and Eve set foot on God's real estate, every living soul has become familiar with the name Jesus Christ People from all walks of life talk about him and eventually come to the realization, whether they personally believe it or not, that he is not just an ordinary man Jesus is a man with problem-solving skills which include the interaction of the mind, the imagination, the heart, and the spirit.

Individuals who accept his method of solving problems by using their intellect and faith and prayer, find solutions to their troubles. Individuals who ignore his methods ultimately fail.

Since the day Jesus walked this earth he has been identified as a mighty counselor, the Son of Man, the Son of God.

Every single one of us who seek lasting solutions to the hell in which we all encounter from time to time need to stop in our tracks, take a deep breath, and upon exhaling the breath of life, return to the basic fundamental truth which sustains life-faith in God.

In Psalm 55, King David, like so many of us today, cried out to God in his greatest hour of need-*"Return unto me the joy of thy salvation."* This was David's last desperate attempt to catch God's attention in dealing with the troubles which were overwhelming him.

King David became the victim of every problem known to man. Some problems were brought to him via other people.

Most problems were self-inflicted by introducing into his life the ugliness of sin.

King David is a perfect illustration of a person who tried over and over again to solve his problems and to overcome lifes obstacles by using his own intellectual power and failed.

It was not until he returned to the basic fundamental biblical truth of exercising faith in God that his sins were forgiven, his problems overcome, and his kingdom restored.

I believe King David's cry is the cry many people express today who by chance or circumstance have been tossed into a turbulent sea of trouble pushing them to such limits of depression and hopelessness that they have by intent or by ignorance eliminated God from their lives *"I Am With You Always"* is a book which will help guide YOU to a deeper faith in God.

You will be reading about people just like yourself who encountered extraordinary incidents which eventually delivered them from their own hell and placed them on a road to the blessings God has promised all of us.

Returning to basic principles of exercising a child-like faith in God has proven to men, women, and children, from all generations that a close fellowship with Jesus Christ leads to the refreshing air and living waters which sustain a blessed life.

"I Am With You Always" does not outline earth-shaking events or lightening answers to prayer; you will not read of highly visible miracles or dynamic events pushing you to the edge of your seat What you will read however, is how twelve police officers who, by a divinely inspired turn of events found themselves on life's "fork

in the road" and unexpectedly encountered the power of a man called Jesus.

May this journal be your reminder that God is alive and well and that he has not in the past, will not today, nor ever in the years to come break his solemn promise, *"I Am With You Always."*

Sergeant Steven L. Rogers

Chapter 1
ALASKA-NEW JERSEY CONNECTION

O fficer William Palata is a man who has never been ashamed to privately and publicly share his deep spiritual convictions and strong belief and devotion to the God he calls Jesus.

Since his early childhood Bill Palata's parents made sure he attended Sunday school classes each week and encouraged him to read his Bible daily and pray every night before he went to sleep

It was during this time in his life that the seeds of faith and the power of prayer were planted in his heart, soul, and spirit Bill's parents, Mary and John Palata, planted spiritual seeds in their son's heart which would be watered in future years by people they would never come to know.

At the age of twenty, Bill Palata became a police officer in one of New Jersey's largest cities During his first few months on the job he met several Christian police officers who shared with him their faith and what they knew to be biblical truths which helped guide them through both peaceful and difficult times at home and at work.

His conversations and fellowship with these officers led him to a closer walk with God Eventually, he accepted Jesus Christ as his Personal Savior.

As a result of becoming more familiar with the Bible and learning more about Jesus Christ, Officer Palata developed an intense desire to share his new found faith with others

1

His opportunity to do this came in 1995 when he was asked by a magazine editor to write an article entitled, "A Closer Walk with God." The editor told him that if the article had substance which could be helpful to people, it would be published.

Several weeks after Bill wrote the article, he submitted it to the magazine editorial board. It was published and public reaction was favorable.

Three months after it was distributed nationwide, Officer Palata, who was sitting behind his desk at police headquarters, was opening some mail and found an interesting letter which stirred his spirit.

Dear Officer Palata, I read your magazine article entitled; "A Closer Walk with God" and I must tell you it moved me greatly. My name is Philip Wilson. I am a prisoner in the Alaska State Penitentiary. I am here because several years ago I committed an armed robbery and shot a police officer. His name is Gerald Barton. After the shooting, I heard the officer had to retire because he is crippled as a result of my shot. I deeply regret what I did. My reason for writing you is to let you know that while in prison I accepted Christ as my Savior. I know that I must pay the penalty for my crime and sin. But I also know Jesus has forgiven me.

My reason for writing you is to ask a favor. Since the time I accepted Jesus into my life I felt a compelling need to personally ask Officer Barton to forgive me for what I did to him. I have tried to reach him several times but the police department won't allow me to talk with him. I know God wants me to seek his forgiveness. I don't know what he will say or how he will react if I ever do get to talk with him.

But my spirit is heavy and I know God wants me to at least try.

If you can help me I humbly ask you to try to reach Officer Barton and tell him my story. I will understand if you do not help. But if you do I will be very greatful. Thanks and may God lead you in this matter. Very truly yours, Philip Wilson, 87987.

After reading Wilson's letter Officer Palata's face became pale and his heart began to beat rapidly. He sat in his chair for almost an hour pondering as to what he should do-attempt to reach the crippled officer and share with him Wilson's letter and risk opening old wounds; or disregard the letter and risk the opportunity of seizing upon a divinely directed mission.

He decided to first pray about the matter. Right there in his office he got on his knees and sought God's guidance Palata learned early in life that before acting on any matter it was wise to first seek God's guidance.

Within forty-five minutes from the moment he folded his hands and began to pray, Palata had his answer The Spirit of God impressed upon his heart to contact the Alaskan Police Officer

Palata knew there was no way he could ignore this divine nudging from the heavenly realm so he picked up his telephone and dialed the Alaska Police Department.

After a police dispatcher answered the phone Bill Palata identified himself and requested to speak with Officer Gerald Barton regarding a personal matter.

The dispatcher explained that Officer Barton was forced to retire on a disability after being shot by a robbery suspect and that he no longer worked for the police department She offered to make an attempt to contact him at his home and request he return Palata's call.

Palata gave the dispatcher his phone number and thanked her. For the next thirty minutes Palata walked around his office, sweated, twiddled his thumbs, and diddled on a pad while waiting for the telephone to ring.

After what seemed to be a very long wait, Officer Palata concluded that he was not going to receive the call from Alaska. He packed his briefcase with some papers and started to walk toward his office door when he was suddenly startled by the phone which began to ring. At first he hesitated to pick it up.

"What if it's this cop who got shot? What am I going to say to him?"

As these and other questions raced through his mind, Palata finally gathered the courage to answer the phone Indeed, it was Officer Gerald Barten calling from Alaska.

After a short introduction, Officer Palata explained the reason why he called by mentioning the letter he received from Wilson.

When Palata finished speaking there was what seemed to be a very long silence on the other end of the phone. Palata thought Barten had hung up on him. Then before he uttered the words "are you there," the voice of Barten's very soft, very broken, and with obvious tears streaming down his face, began to speak.

Officer Gerald Barten explained to Palata that he was a cop who loved his job But he was also a man with no peace.

4

Barten was living in the fast lane, drinking, partying, and doing wild things. He explained that one night a Christian police officer spoke with him about Christ. "I mocked God and cursed the cop who tried to talk sense into me," he explained. "A few hours later I got shot."

Barten went on to explain that while he was dying in a hospital bed he had a dream about God In his dream Jesus Christ told him that if he wanted his life restored he had to forgive the very man who put him in the "death bed " When he awakened, he was in turmoil He thought he could never forgive the man who nearly took his life.

As the days in the hospital became months, a police chaplain visited him almost daily and explained that Jesus Christ loved him so much he spared his life for a divine purpose. When he asked the chaplain what he thought the purpose was the chaplain replied that he did not know but that when he (Barten) would do two things God would reveal to him what that purpose was. Barten then asked the chaplain what the two things were that he needed to do. The chaplain replied, "First, accept Jesus Christ as your Savior. Second, forgive your assailant." Barten grew angry and asked the chaplain to leave.

Several weeks passed and after realizing he could no longer fight the will of God, Barten called for the chaplain and asked him to forgive him for losing his temper. The chaplain told the young officer he understood and offered to pray with him

Barten accepted Jesus as his Savior but refused to forgive his assailant. The chaplain did not push the issue and told Barten he would have to work this out with God on a one-to-one basis.

There were times Barten struggled with the idea of getting in-touch with Wilson but he couldn't bring himself to that point. He decided to pray that God would give him the strength to forgive.

Gerald Barten's prayer was answered when Palata made his call to him. Barten explained to Palata that he knew what he had to do-call Wilson and forgive him.

Palata and Barten spoke about how God used a cop (Palata) nearly 3,000 miles away from Alaska to get a message to another cop (Barten). They prayed with each other and thanked God for beginning the process of healing the wounds between two mortal enemies.

When the conversation ended Palata was about to leave his office when he noticed one more piece of mail on his desk.

After removing a small piece of paper from the envelope, he unfolded it and read a bible scripture typed on the paper- *"well done thou good and faithful servant."* signed, anonymous.

Chapter 2
THE PIECE OF PAPER

For nearly ten years Baltimore City police officer John Stuart had been writing magazine articles about the need for law enforcement agencies to appoint chaplains to police agencies He believed such appointments would give police officers an opportunity to deal with their problems from a spiritual perspective

John Stuart's publications, editorials, and commentaries on topics related to law enforcement and the bible gained him a degree of fame in the criminal justice community. His magazine articles were widely read and distributed throughout the United States

On December 14, 1996, Officer Stuart was in a local church thinking about how many police officers and their families needed to hear the salvation message of Jesus Christ and the healing power of the word of God. He looked up at the altar and asked God to bless him with a way he could reach thousands of law enforcement officers with the messages and material he was presently publishing via news print. What this young officer had on his mind was to host a talk radio program dedicated to law enforcement and addressing criminal justice issues from a biblical perspective.

Soon after leaving the church he went home and walked into his den where he opened his bible. He read two scriptures which had profound impact on him. The first was chapter one, verse 19, in the book of Isaiah; *"If ye be willing and obedient you shall eat the good of the land."*

The other scripture was the book of James, chapter 5, verse 16; *"The effectual fervent prayer of a righteous man availeth much."*

Officer Stuart believed that God was telling him something via these two biblical passages. Hence, he placed his bible down on a table and began to pray.

While praying about his desire to broadcast the "good news" via radio, Stuart had no idea that an event which would have profound impact on his life was unfolding in a small dinner on a highway in New Jersey, nearly 400 miles away from Baltimore.

While on patrol in the early morning hours of December 14, 1996, New Jersey police sergeant Andrew Gilbert stopped by a restaurant in his community for a cup of coffee.

While sipping his hot Java, he pulled from his coat pocket a folded piece of paper his wife had given him the night before. The piece of paper was actually an article she had cut out of a magazine she read earlier in the week.

Officer Gilbert read a few short paragraphs, folded the paper again, and placed it in an ashtray which was on his table. After he swallowed his last mouthful of coffee he paid the waitress and went back to his patrol car and drove off.

Before the waitress who served Officer Gilbert could get to his table to clean it, a hungry customer entered the restaurant and sat at the table Officer Gilbert had occupied minutes earlier.

The waitress offered this man a clean table but he refused, telling her that he comes to this restaurant often and always sits in the same spot.

As the man waited for his cup of coffee he noticed the folded paper in the ashtray. Since he had nothing else to do, he picked up the paper, unfolded it and began to read its contents. The first words he noticed were the title of an article written by Police Officer John Stuart. His curiosity heightened and he began to read the entire magazine article which told of dramatic events occurring in the police profession with biblical perspectives as a main theme

After drinking his coffee and having a small bite to eat the man folded the magazine article and placed it in his pocket. He paid his bill, got into his car, and began his thirty minute drive to his New York City office where he managed a radio station.

At 10:00am the radio station manager attended a previously scheduled staff meeting with his news and editorial board. Among the group of men and women sitting on the board was a special feature writer named Doris Harris. Mrs. Harris specialized in producing feature radio stories on interesting people and events with unique biblical perspectives.

During this meeting the station manager told Mrs. Harris that he had read a magazine article written by a police officer in Baltimore which she may be interested in. He handed her the piece of paper he stuffed in his pocket earlier in the day and assigned her to contact Officer Stuart.

Two days after this meeting, Mrs. Harris contacted Officer Stuart and advised him that she was interested in doing a news story on his publications and offered to interview him, via the telephone. He accepted her offer and conducted a ten minute news interview exploring his background, his work as a police officer and his desire to reach as many law enforcement officers as possible with the salvation message of Jesus Christ.

The interview was aired that evening from New York to Washington, D.C As soon as the radio broadcast ended, the telephones in the radio station began to ring and people from throughout the entire listening area praised the station and the police officer for the broadcast.

A few minutes before the station was about to close for the evening, one more call came in. A man named Donald Gilbert from New York City asked for Mrs. Harris and personally commended her for the interview she conducted with Officer Stuart. He then went on to tell her to inform Officer Stuart that a check would be in the mail to the radio station in an amount sufficient enough for him to air a fifteen minute broadcast once a day for the entire year.

Two weeks later the check arrived and Officer Stuart taped more than 365 programs that year. His words reached a listening audience of more than one million people, proclaiming the goodness of God and the need for police officers and their family members to reach out to Jesus Christ for peace in times of trouble.

Officer John Stuart's faith in Christ led to the fulfillment of his dream and an answer to his prayer.

One footnote· Donald Gilbert is the brother of Officer Andrew Gilbert, the police officer who originally folded the piece of paper and placed it in the ashtray

Chapter 3
HIGHWAY TO HEAVEN

It was a crisp cool night when off-duty police officers Henry Martin and Rocco Smalls left a church meeting in Willow Grove, Pennsylvania to head back to their homes in New Jersey. Both officers, who are Christians, were invited to speak at a womens prayer conference not far from the Naval Air Station located in that community.

Officers Martin and Smalls had been police officers for nearly 20 years. Both officers were very outspoken on issues related to their profession, the government, and the church. In 1995, they began to accept speaking invitations from Christian and civic organizations throughout the nation.

On March 7, 1996, both officers left their southern New Jersey homes at 6:00pm and headed toward Willow-Grove in Henry Martin's new blue Plymouth van. Martin was so proud of his walk with Christ and what he was doing on that day with Smalls, he put a sign on both sides of the van which read, "God Squad."

The trip to the Pennsylvania church where the conference was being held went smooth. Traffic was light, the weather was good, and they arrived about 30 minutes ahead of schedule.

After a short snack at a church member's home, the officers were escorted to the church conference room where approximately 65 men and women were waiting for them.

After being introduced to the crowd both officers took their turn sharing the need for people to pray for their local police officers. When they finished their presentations, the officers received a standing ovation from the crowd.

When the applause ended the church pastor thanked the officers for traveling to his community and offered a prayer of thanks for the blessing bestowed upon everyone that evening. As the pastor concluded his remarks he prayed, "Lord, if there is one police officer, just one, who is in need of your love, your Holy Spirit, and your divine guidance to the Cross, let him find the path to your arms this evening." Amen.

At 11:00pm Officer Martin and Smalls said good-bye to everyone and began their journey back to New Jersey.

At 11:25pm, Officer Martin, who was driving, decided to take a short cut and entered the Pennsylvania Turnpike at a different location than that of the one he used to arrive in Pennsylvania.

As the officers traveled east to New Jersey, both of them noticed that the "shortcut" ended up being a longer way back home Martin remarked to his partner that since the road was nearly empty he could make up some time by going a little faster. So he accelerated his van.

Not two minutes after accelerating from 50mph to 80mph, Henry Martin noticed in his rear view mirror a car speeding toward his van. As the car got closer, he noticed two red lights flashing and then what sounded like a siren. It was a Pennsylvania State Police car.

"Oh boy," Smalls remarked. "You better pray about this one Henry, you were speeding."

After the van and the police car pulled over to the highway shoulder, the trooper began his walk toward the driver's door. Martin, who was looking at the trooper through the van's side view mirror noticed that he momentarily stopped, pointed his flashlight onto the sign which read "God Squad," and proceeded his walk.

"License please. Where are you guys headed?" asked the six-foot 190 pound trooper.

As Henry was handing the trooper his license and explaining to him where he was going, the trooper suddenly interrupted and asked, "What's this God Squad?"

"Now he will think we are nuts," said Smalls so only Martin could hear him.

Henry Martin explained to the very attentive state trooper what he and Smalls were doing in Pennsylvania. When he finished speaking, the trooper, who didn't utter one word and seemed to be in a trance, asked both men to exit the van and to get into the police car Smalls told his partner that he said too much and that the trooper must have thought they were imposters and not cops. Martin did not reply.

When all three men got into the police car Martin and Smalls sat in the back seat and the trooper sat behind the steering wheel.

"Listen," began the trooper. "I believe you guys are cops and I believe you were here to speak at a church group I also believe that somehow God is dealing with me. I'm under a lot of pressure. I just got married and my wife tells me that she sees me in distress and that she is praying for me. I keep on fighting her words and I keep on resisting this tug inside of me. Anyway, tonight, before

I came to work, I decided to ask God to show me what my wife is talking about.

I went over there to that overpass you just drove past and parked my police car and in my own way prayed for God to help me. A few minutes after I said those words I looked up and saw your van with that sign "God Squad" on it flying by me like a rocket. I'm convinced God heard my prayer," he concluded with a broken voice and eyes swelling with tears

Officer Martin and Smalls prayed with the state trooper right there and then on the highway.

After saying good-bye, both New Jersey officers went back to the van and drove off praising God for what had just occurred. Moments later Officer Smalls recalled the prayer of the church pastor before they left the conference. *"Lord,if there is one police officer, just one, who is in need of your love, your Holy Spirit, and your divine guidance to the Cross, let him find the path to your arms this evening. Amen."*

Chapter 4

DANIEL

Officer Steven Wallace is a man who has always made it very clear to both friend and foe that his love for Christ and his desire to help anyone who crossed his path by introducing them to the Gospel of Jesus Christ was unwavering

Wallace, who is 40 years old and married makes it a point to tell people that he is far from perfect, not the best example of a "good" Christian, and could probably do more to advance the cause of Christ. "I do know enough to get on my knees and say Lord forgive me for my sins," he tells people.

It was not unusual for Steven Wallace to participate in a celebration of America's religions at a New Jersey mall in April of 1996. He always took advantage of opportunities to share the good news of the Bible; so what better way to reach hundreds of people at one time, he thought.

The event, sponsored by mall management, was easy to participate in. Any person or organization who wished to distribute literature or material about a bona-fide religious organization or cause would be able to set up a small booth in the mall and encourage shoppers to listen to their message and accept their material

After Officer Wallace applied to participate in this event his request was approved and he and his lovely wife Donna set up a small booth in the mall on April 4th. They displayed bibles, books related to police officers and God, and other material related to Christian principles.

Both Wallace and his wife were excited at the location of their booth-right in front of Macy's Department Store- the place where most mall shoppers visited. Hence, thousands if not hundreds of people had to walk by their booth before entering or leaving the giant store.

The couple's excitement was short-lived. A man in his middle thirties and who represented an eastern religious order approached Officer Wallace and advised him that the spot he had erected his booth on was reserved for his organization and that he had to move.

Officer Wallace resisted until the man produced a document proving that mall management promised his religious order the spot in front of Macy's. Reluctantly, and without further discussion the young police officer and his wife began to take down all the material they had just put up.

In their quest to find a new location, mall management summoned them to the general managers office where Mrs.Mary Thompson, the event coordinator, advised the couple that the only space available for them to erect their display was in a corner area near the restrooms. "No! Absolutely not!" protested Wallace.

After Mrs.Thompson gave the officer an ultimatum to either set up the booth at that location or set up no booth at all Wallace shut his mouth and proceeded to walk to the restroom area.

When the couple completed setting up their "new" booth, Donna and Steven Wallace quietly sat in two chairs watching hundreds of people travel in and out of the restrooms. Not one person stopped to review the material they displayed. Officer Wallace remarked to his wife several times, "I knew this would be a bad location." What Wallace and his wife didn't know was that God was doing something on the other side of the mall in preparation for a chain of events which would eventually have impact on the lives of the Wallaces' and a few other people.

Sixty-three year old Daniel O'Mara was a loner. He and his wife Angela had serious marital problems and his life was as empty as a dry well

The mall was Daniel's escape from reality. He would visit this place every day to walk endless miles with his mind racing to nowhere.

On April 4, 1996, Daniel was having a very difficult day. He was at his wit's end and he could not find peace of mind. He was feeling so empty and so void he did not want to live anymore

Everyday Daniel visited the mall he entered through Macy's department store. He used the same route so often everyone in the store greeted him as he walked through their separate departments. But this day, April 4, would be a day which would disrupt Daniels routine and forever change his life As usual, Daniel parked his car near Macy's and began his 500-foot walk toward the huge department store entrance

A man who recognized Daniel walking from the parking lot to the store called his name It was Ned Thompson, his neighbor. Ned was shopping and when he returned to his car he found that his battery went dead.

Daniel approached Ned and assessed the problem. He got his car and pulled it next to his neighbor's vehicle and connected battery cables to both of them. In a few short minutes Ned's car started.

After exchanging a few kind words with each other Ned pulled his car out of the parking space he was occupying and drove off Daniel then pulled his car into Ned's former space and once again began his walk toward Macy's

As Daniel began his walk, a large cloud hovering overhead burst wide open and a down pour of rain descended on the area. Daniel was not prepared for this change in weather and quickly ran to the nearest doorway for cover.

Although the doorway had a sign on it which warned "Employees Entrance Only," Daniel decided to enter it anyway and walked down the long hallway toward the store inside the mall.

While this was going on, Angela O'Mara, Daniel's wife, was on the other side of town, in a small church praying for God to touch her husband. For many years Daniel's family and friends tried to speak with him about the Bible and about Jesus Christ, but he rejected their words and resisted their attempts to convince him that there was no other way to solve his problems but God's way.

Back at the mall, when he finally reached the inner doorway entrance, Daniel walked directly into the booth Officer Wallace and his wife had set up.

"Hey partner, looks like you got a little wet." exclaimed Wallace. "Yea, a little. You a cop? What this God stuff?" asked and inquisitive O'Mara.

Steven Wallace seized the moment and carefully explained to Daniel why he and his wife Donna were at the mall. He shared with this tired elderly man a message

18

about Jesus Christ. The sixty-five-year-old politely listened but said not a word until Wallace finished.

"Look, I don't need this God stuff. I've committed so much sin not even the devil wants anything to do with me. God would be wasting his time in dealing with me," he said

Daniel continued to speak with Wallace about his family problems, his loneliness, his unexplainable void and constant sinking feeling. He told the young officer and his wife that he liked them and perhaps one day they would meet again.

"Do you really want to meet again?" asked Wallace. "Sure, sure I do, I can chat with you You're not one of those Jesus freaks," replied a cautious Daniel.

"I'll tell you what Dan; Donna and I will be at the Saint Marks Church in Bloomfield next Sunday. I'm scheduled to speak to the congregation at 11·00am. How about coming to see us?"

"I don't like to go to church. I'll meet you afterwards; how's that?" replied Daniel. "Whatever is good for you, I'll see you then," said Wallace as he and his wife said goodbye to their new friend

Meanwhile, back at the O'Mara home, Mrs. O'Mara received a telephone call from a friend who was told that a police officer was going to be a guest speaker at St. Marks Church on Sunday. The neighbor wanted to know if she knew of any police officers whom she could invite. Mrs. O'Mara told her friend that a neighbor who lived two houses from her was a policeman and that she would invite him and his wife.

When Daniel returned home he noticed his bedroom door closed. That meant his wife was praying He respected her prayer time and never interrupted her. But every time he saw the door closed he felt a pulling of his spirit as if something or someone was telling him to join her.

Sunday morning arrived with a warm breeze and beautiful sunshine. When Officer Steven Wallace and his wife Donna arrived at St. Mark's the parking lot was full and several local police officers were inside the church Mrs. O'Mara had accompanied her neighbors to the service and was sitting in the balcony.

After the pastor introduced Steven Wallace, the young officer spoke for about twenty-five minutes. He talked of God's healing power, the anointing of police officers as written in Romans, Chapter 13, and the love Jesus has for all people, no matter what color, age, or background. When he finished his presentation, he said, "If there is anyone in this room this morning who knows he or she is on an empty road going nowhere I urge you to change the direction of your life by coming forward as an act of faith and asking Jesus Christ into your life."

For fifteen minutes Wallace and the entire congregation had their heads bowed. The church became very silent. Suddenly, out of nowhere a disheveled looking man, unshaven, dirty clothes, and tears dripping down his face began to walk very so slowly down the center isle of the church toward the altar. It was Daniel O'Mara.

When this broken hearted man reached the altar where Officer Wallace was standing, Mrs. O'Mara, in disbelief, began to cry and silently thanked God for the deliverance of her husband who she had prayed for so long.

Wallace looked at O'Mara and with the help of the church pastor prayed with him. Within minutes Daniel O'Mara, at the age of sixty-five accepted Jesus Christ as his Lord and Savior.

Several weeks after that day Daniel and his wife attended church services regularly and once again became a happy couple. Daniel even helped out with the church youth ministry from time to time.

One year later Officer Wallace was in his patrol car cruising along the west side of his community when he passed a small grocery store and observed a commotion of people near the front door. He decided to pull his car into the parking lot.

As soon as he exited his vehicle a man ran to him and screamed, "I think a man in there is having a heart attack!" Officer Wallace immediately radioed police headquarters for an ambulance and ran into the store where he saw the elderly man on the floor, face down gasping for air.

As the officer turned the man over, he and the victim stared directly into each others eyes and in a final gasp of air the man uttered, "It's time for me to go home. I will never forget you." Minutes later Daniel O'Mara died in the arms of Officer Steven Wallace.

Today, Mrs. O'Mara works at her church in a ministry for the elderly. Officer Wallace and his wife Donna continue to spread the "good news" to the law enforcement community. And Daniel O'Mara no longer walks the halls of a mall. Instead, he walks on the streets of the city whose builder and maker is God.

Chapter 5

THE HOUSE THAT JESUS BUILT

After two-years of marriage and living in a one bedroom apartment it was time for Officer William Mathias and his wife Wendy to move into larger living quarters. After all, they were expecting their first child and needed the space.

The thirty-one year old police officer and his wife are devout Christians. They are liked by many people because they are balanced in their thinking and never push the church or God on anyone who did not want to hear about it.

They do however have a strong belief in the power of prayer. Bill often tells people that if a person truly wanted to see the movement of God all one needed to do was to be persistent in prayer.

On July 7, 1996, Bill and Wendy Mathias went house hunting. Previous to this day they had been traveling every weekend to a new part of New Jersey looking at various kinds of one-family houses. This day however would lead them to the end of their journey.

While traveling south on the Garden State Parkway from Newark, New Jersey, the young police officer asked his wife, "what kind of house are you looking for, Wendy?" She told him she had been praying to God to give her the means to buy a single family home with a sunken living room, ceiling fans, fireplace, den, three bedrooms, and a nice size yard.

Officer Mathias took a long look at his wife and replied, "remember you are married to a cop, not a doctor." A few minutes after this short conversation Bill noticed his fuel gauge was registering low. He pulled off the parkway at the next exit and drove into an Amoco gas station

As his car was being fueled his wife noticed a billboard across the street from them. It was an advertisement about single family homes being built in New Brunswick, New Jersey, about 45 minutes from where they were The ad offered homes, not yet built, at preconstruction prices.

Wendy urged Bill to take the ride to Brunswick to take a look at what was being offered. He agreed and began his journey south.

About an hour later the couple arrived at the construction site and observed five beautiful single family homes being used as models for perspective buyers to look at. At first, the couple felt that the prices of the homes were beyond their financial range but they decided to look at them anyway.

Bill and Wendy Mathias went into the visitors' office and registered their names. They then visited the first model home. As soon as they entered it a chill ran up and down both their backs. What they saw was the exact description of the type of home Wendy described to Bill when they were at the gas station.

Instead of looking at the other model homes the couple went directly to the sales office and inquired as to the price of the home which caught their eyes

"Two-hundred thousand dollars and the home is yours," said a sales woman. "All you need is $10,000 down," she added The couple stood stunned for a while

Their fear that the price would be too high for them to handle became a reality.

The woman interrupted Bill and Wendy's thoughts and further said, "Look, if you give me a check for $100.00 as a deposit, I will hold that home for 15 days. If at that time you cannot buy it, you get your money back."

Bill was ready to say thanks but no thanks when Wendy immediately said, "Okay," with a stunned husband looking at her.

After Wendy wrote out the $100 00 check and handed it to the sales woman, the couple got back into their car and began their ride home.

"Where are we going to get ten-thousand dollars and a mortgage that big Wendy?"

"Bill, have faith. I am convinced God is going to work something out for us?"

When the couple arrived home they counted all of their assets, including a piggy-bank filled with one-dollar bills.

Between savings accounts, bonds, and a checking account they added up about $7,000.00 which could be used toward the down payment

"We need ten-thousand dollars. Where do we find the other $3,000?" asked a distress Bill.

"Well, my dear husband, here is your chance to practice what you tell everyone else to do?"

"What's that?" asked a curious Bill Mathias. "Pray," replied Wendy.

The couple conversed for a short time and agreed that this was a matter for God to deal with They had been faithful in the little things which God blessed them with and truly believed that God with give them a greater blessing They went to sleep with the dream of their lifetime on their minds.

The next day Officer Mathias went to work and was assigned to patrol the east side of his township. His road sergeant told him to keep a close eye on a construction site where some vandalism was taking place.

About 9·30am, Bill Mathias pulled his patrol car into the construction site and met one of the foreman.

"Hi officer, how are you today?" asked the foreman

"Fine, just fine. My boss told me about vandals causing you some problems. I thought I would come down and take a look," replied Mathias.

"That's fine with me. Hey, while I got you here, do you know of anyone looking for a part-time job?"

"No, not really. What kind of work do you have in mind?" asked Mathias.

"Well, its maintenance work. You see I have these condos going up and when the construction workers are finished with each unit they have a bad habit of using the new toilets. The problem is that the plumbing is not yet connected to the water main. Get the picture?"

"Yes, I sure do. I don't know who you will get to do that. How much are you paying?"

"I figured there are about two hundred toilets. So for cleaning all of them I'll offer someone $1,000.00. It's dirty work and time consuming you know," explained the foreman.

Bill Mathias couldn't believe his ears. The man offered one third of the money he and Wendy needed to add to the down payment on their new home. "Look, I need the money. I'll do it!" exclaimed Mathias.

On that very evening Officer Mathias and his wife began the long hard job of cleaning out nearly 200 toilets filled with human waste from 5:00pm each night to 1:00am in the morning for the next 12 days.

On day twelve the site foreman handed Mathias a check in the amount of one thousand dollars. He was so impressed with the speed and cleanliness of their work he offered them a permanent "maintenance job."The couple thanked him but turned the offer down.

The next day the Mathias' rested. They prayed and talked for several hours Both of them knew they were $2,000.00 short of the amount they needed and had no idea where it would come from. At 11:00pm, exhausting all avenues and trying to think of every way possible to get the money they needed, the couple finally concluded that they would not get the home because they were short two-thousand dollars. Distressed and disappointed Wendy went to bed

Bill also was getting ready to go to bed when the door bell rang. "Who in the world could that be at this hour," he thought.

When he opened the door he recognized the visitor to be a man he met several years ago at a local church service

"Bob, Bob Henion?" asked Mathias.

"Yes Bill, it's me. Please forgive me for stopping by at this hour."

"No problem Bob, is anything wrong?"
As Bob was sharing his recent experiences as a missionary in Africa. Wendy awakened and joined them.

She remembered Bob Henion when they all met at

a church service in 1992. Henion was so impressed with Bill's zeal for the Gospel he told the young officer and his wife that he would never forget them. Obviously he kept his word. Bob Henion began to explain.

"About fifteen days ago I was in deep prayer. Interestingly, God brought both of you to my mind. I prayed and asked God what it was that he wanted me to do regarding you two. After all, I met you only once, a few years ago, and now your names came to my mind out of the blue. Anyway, the Lord placed it upon my heart to deliver you this envelope. Do not open it until I leave. Believe me, I know this sounds strange but it's for real "

The couple was dumbfounded. When they began to ask Henion some questions regarding the envelope he immediately got up from the chair and told them he had to leave. As he said goodbye he told the Mathias's that God truly loved them.

Wendy and her husband were perplexed. Nonetheless they knew that Henion was a man of God and not a nut. They concluded that he must have had a strong conviction regarding this matter.

"Oh well, let's see what's in the envelope," Wendy remarked.

As Bill Mathias opened the envelope he could not believe his eyes. He was so stunned he couldn't speak. His wife grabbed it from him and she too became stunned after looking at it. In the little envelope they counted twenty one-hundred dollar bills-the amount they needed to add to the total amount they already had for the down payment on the home they wanted.The couple cried together and fell to their knees thanking God for what they knew was a gift from heaven.

The next day Bill and Wendy returned to Brunswick and handed the sales woman the $10,000 down payment she requested.She told them the house would be completed in about seven months.

As Bill and Wendy were exiting the office Wendy stopped and turned toward the woman and asked, "By the way, what will our new address be?" The woman replied, "7 Faith Drive."

Chapter 6
THE COPS & THE ANGLES

Like a forest fire that dies down and is rekindled by a slow passing wind, the violence of the mob rose once more and erupted into a full flamed conflagration of noise and rioting. Beer and wine bottles smashed against walls, teenage boys were fighting over girls, and a boiling rage fed the flames of violence as if gasoline was thrown on a blazing inferno.

Officer Steven Rogers and his partner Phil knew it was time to make their move. For months they had been investigating and surveilling an area of their community where major alcohol and drug activity was taking place.

After months of exhaustive interviews and receiving information from informants, they knew exactly when and where a meeting of "Mr.Big" the dealer of the illegal booze and drugs-and a group of buyers would be.

The "cave" was the place to watch on this warm and muggy summer evening. Both officers surveilled the "cave" from a small riverbed about 100 yards from its entrance. They observed a lot of activity. For nearly two hours teenagers of all ages came and went, buying alcohol and drugs from Mr. Big.

As the officers waited for the crowd of teens in the cave to leave, thus giving them the opportunity to raid it with minimal danger to themselves and others, it appeared that they were not going anywhere.

As a result, the officers had to make a critical decision-either raid the cave now or walk away missing a one time chance to bag Mr. Big.

Both policemen realized the danger that existed. The last thing they wanted to see was someone get hurt or killed. There was no telling what kind of weapons Mr.Big had. And knowing what the mixture of alcohol and drugs can do to the mind, the potential for an explosive situation was very possible.

However, they balanced their thoughts on the danger along with their knowledge of what Mr. Big had done in the past to young people and their families. Hence, the decision was made to move in now!

Both officers hid near a low riverbed concealing themselves until they were absolutely ready to charge the cave. As they waited, they prayed Psalm 91- "For he shall give his angles charge over thee." It is this Psalm in which God promises protection over his people.

A few minutes later the officers moved in on the cave and immediately swooped down on Mr.Big and more than two dozen drunken and drug crazed teenagers.

Ready for a violent confrontation the officers yelled, "POLICE FREEZE!" To their surprise no one moved. The teens and Mr. Big froze as if they were in shock and in great fear.

The policemen apprehended twenty-five suspects, some adults, most teenagers. When additional police units arrived at the crime scene all of the suspects were transported to police headquarters where the juveniles were turned over to their parents and adults placed on bail.

Mr.Big was placed in jail because he could not come up with the 5,000 cash bail.

Twelve days later all the adults, including Mr Big appeared in court to answer the charges. Through a plea bargain agreement with all the adults accept Mr Big all pleaded guilty and were fined. Mr. Big's charges of distributing drugs to minors was referred to a grand jury He was arraigned and pleaded not guilty. Because he could not make bail he was once again sent to jail

As the court officers were walking down a hallway escorting Mr. Big to his cell they unexpectedly came face to face with Officer Steve.

"You liar, you no good lying cop,"screamed a violent Mr Big

"What did I lie about? Tell me what did I lie about?" asked Officer Steve.

"The number of cops at the cave I'm not blind. There were at least fifty of you there. You told the judge only you and your partner were at the cave. You liar!" Before Steve could reply, the officers pulled Mr. Big away.

"What was that all about?" asked Phil as he approached Steve.

"I don't know. He said I lied about the number of cops in the cave."

"That interesting," replied Phil. One of the teenage girls called me a liar also She said there were at least "fifty-cops" with us.

As both officers began to laugh and joke about the suspects state of mind they suddenly stopped and realized that this was nothing to joke about. After some reflection on the entire case both remembered that just before they raided the cave they prayed Psalm 91- "For he shall give his angels charge over thee . ."

31

Chapter 7
UNTO THY HANDS I COMMIT MY SPIRIT

Police Lieutenant John Grover was a tough street cop who loved his job, his family, and above all God. For generations his family lived, worked, and grew together in the same community.

John Grover was raised a Catholic. His parents gave him the best biblical instruction any young man could have.

At the age of thirty-five he sought a deeper and closer relationship with God and started attending an evangelical church. He soon accepted Jesus Christ as his Personal Savior.

For a period of three years this young officer studied the Bible and gained a tremendous amount of insight and knowledge about heaven, hell, life, death, and God's plan for the salvation of man.

He attended church twice a week, became a Sunday school teacher, and led several Sunday services in churches throughout the nation when invited by local pastors to speak

Wherever John Grover spoke about Christ people listened carefully. He was, as one man put it, "a very gifted police officer and speaker."

Although John Grover was successful in convincing hundreds of people all over America to read the Bible and accept Jesus Christ as their Savior, he had a tremendous burden on his heart for his family.

John tried to talk with his parents about the Gospels, but they resisted and told him several times they weren't interested in being "converted" However, as days became weeks, and weeks months, John continued to pray for his parents daily. For the first time he saw some fruits of his prayers in February of 1985, when his mother began to ask him a lot questions about the Bible. By April of that same year John's mother accepted Jesus Christ as her Personal Savior

John's father Sam was more difficult to deal with. He was raised an Irish Catholic and no way he was going to convert to the Protestant faith. "That would be sinful," he use to say. But this did not discourage John. Everyday he would get on his knees and pray for his dad.

On June 1, 1985, Sam Grover asked his son about King David and the book of Psalms- a remarkable breakthrough, thought John.

He told his dad what the Psalms was all about and gave him some background on the King. John then gave his dad a book entitled-The Treasury of David-by Charles Spurgeon. That was the first and last time Sam Grover asked his son anything about the Bible.

From time to time John would drop a word or two here and there with his father about the Bible, but Sam would just listen and not say a word.

On June 21, 1986, John Grover was patrolling the streets of his city when he received a call from the police dispatcher to respond to the local hospital and see a doctor in the emergency room immediately.

Without asking questions, the young Lieutenant automatically put his patrol car red lights and sirens on and raced to St John's Hospital.

When he arrived he met Doctor Bill Mark who told him that his father had been visiting a friend and fell down while walking in a hallway. He had broken his hip and had to be immediately operated on.

When the police officer asked to see his dad the doctor told him he would be in the recovery room in about three hours. John's mother soon arrived and both of them patiently waited and prayed for the recovery of their devoted father and husband.

Several hours later Mr. Grover was wheeled on a stretcher from the operating room to the intensive care unit. Dr. Mark met John and his mother and told them the situation was bad. Sam Grover was in very critical condition. He was on life support.

As the day became night, John and his mother could only communicate with Mr. Grover by making hand signals.

John noticed that his father was struggling to tell him something. Finally, after several signals with both hands and fingers he realized what his dad was communicating to him.

To say the least, John was stunned. His father wanted him to have the doctors remove the life support system. He wanted to risk the chance of living without the machinery hooked up to him. He knew his father was well aware that he could never live without the life support system. Yet, his father did not deserve to die without dignity John Grover was now facing a moral and ethical dilemma.

After consulting with two doctors and speaking with his mother John went off to a small room and prayed for God to give him wisdom in addressing this situation. The one biblical scripture which he continued to recall was from the Proverbs; "there is safety in the multitude of counselors."

Hence, John decided to make a number of calls to very committed Christian friends and his pastor.

Everyone he spoke with agreed that if life cannot be sustained naturally, after attempts are made artificially to revive someone, the decision for the victim is very clear.

John went to see his father, alone. He spoke with him and wanted to be sure his father knew what he was saying. He also wanted to make sure his dad received Jesus into his life. John Grover gave his dad a final salute and farewell. He then went to get his mother who gave her beloved husband a final loving hug and kiss goodbye Moments later John Grover gave the doctor permission to remove the life support system from his father only if he thought he could breathe on his own. The doctor removed the tubes and five minutes later Sam Grover died

John Grover and his mother were deeply saddened and distressed. But preparing for a funeral and contacting friends and family kept them occupied until the day of the funeral.

On the night of his father's death, John Grover was at his home sitting on a wooden chair near his fire place. He had one thing on his mind. "Did my father make it to heaven? Did he really accept Jesus into his life? He asked for the book of Psalms, he asked about David, he asked so many questions, but he never showed any signs of his relationship with Christ," John said to himself over and over again. John was haunted and depressed over these questions he believed he would never find answers to

Before retiring to bed, John Grover stared into the fire place and asked God to give him an answer to his questions related to his father. He got up from his chair and reached into his bookshelf and pulled out the Treasury of David, the book he had given his father several months before he died.

When he began to open the book, a note fell to the floor. When John Grover read its contents, his eyes swelled into a river of tears The note read, *"Dear Son, I want you to know that if I never get a chance to tell you, I leave this letter for you to know that I accepted Jesus Christ as my Savior on the 21st day of June 1985. Thank you for showing me the way back home."*

John Grover's prayer was answered God showed him that his dad was in Heaven

It is interesting to note that Sam Grover died exactly one year to the day-June 21-that he accepted Jesus into his life. His final words on the little note he left for his son to read was, *"Unto thy hands I commit my spirit."*

Chapter 8

MOVING A MOUNTAIN

CHAPTERS 8 THROUGH 12 ARE PERSONAL STORIES FROM THE AUTHOR

It has been said by many people from all walks of life that God can move a mountain. In my case he did just that when I decided to become a police officer in the Township of Nutley, New Jersey.

More than twenty-years ago I decided that I wanted to enter the law enforcement profession by becoming a police officer in a township called Nutley, which is located in New Jersey. I wanted to work there because of that police departments fine reputation.

It was always my desire to help improve the lives of people by being part of a team of men and women dedicated to keeping our streets safe from criminal elements. Becoming a cop was the way I knew I could fulfill this desire.

In 1976, one year after I was honorably discharged from the United States Air Force, I become a police officer in the City of East Orange, New Jersey. Two years later I had an opportunity to become a police officer in the town I really wanted to work in-Nutley, New Jersey.

I had learned that Nutley officials were in the process of hiring probationary officers to fill some vacancies until a civil service police examination was held. So I immediately applied for one of the jobs and to my surprise was hired within two months.

Several months had passed and my probationary period as a patrolman was drawing to a close. Therefore, I applied for the civil service examination and waited for the test to be administered.

Although the possibility of failing the test concerned me, my faith in God gave me a peace and confidence I had never felt before. I believe that my new found faith in biblical promises as a result of my partner leading me to a personal relationship with Jesus Christ had strengthened my confidence like at no other time in my life.

In my zeal I told everyone who enquired as to how I thought I would do on the test that I was sure the Lord would help me pass the examination.

Of course, my response was met with raised eyebrows and funny looks from people who labeled me a "Jesus freak " In fact, some officers made a number of wise cracks at me and predicted I would fail the test. What started as a challenge for me became a direct challenge to the sovereignty and power of Jesus Christ.

As examination day came closer, I found myself becoming distressed and depressed because I learned from police department friends that I would be competing against hundreds of men and women from throughout New Jersey who were seeking the very job I wanted. And adding to my worries, I also learned that Nutley officials were hiring only one person from the list of candidates who passed the test. That one person would be the individual who scored highest on the examination.

I prayed night and day for peace of mind and for the ability to not only pass the test but to attain the highest score in order to retain my job. There was one

Psalm particularly that I prayed daily-Psalm 75; "For promotion cometh not from the east, nor from the west, nor from the south. But God is the judge:he putteth down one and setteth up another."

Each time I prayed my confidence grew. But my good feelings were short lived. One problem I faced was the increasing persecution at work. Every day numerous officers would criticize my deep commitment to God. Some would call me vicious names because I refused to bar-hop with them. Others would paste magazine photos of nude women on my locker with the words "sex is where it's all at" written across the photo. Between the foul language and name calling it was made clear to me that some people wanted me to fail the test because I was not going to be part of their click.

The worst persecution I faced was the day when I walked into a squad room and a superior officer tore into me for talking to another cop about Christ. He grabbed a Bible I had on my desk, called me a Jesus freak, and wiped his buttocks with it. This one single act of defiance against God cut me to the heart. It's a scene I will never forget.

Many times I wanted to shout back at the evil people taunting me. But God, through the power of the Holy Spirit would speak to my inner soul and say, "Be still and know that I am God."

Examination day finally arrived. I was as ready as I could ever be and felt I had done a good job preparing for the test. In addition, I did a lot of praying. I thought things would calm down now but I was wrong.The persecution did not end; in fact, it intensified.

One by one fellow workers made a mockery of God, my faith, the Bible, and anything that had to do with Jesus. I finally broke my silence and warned them that God is not mocked and neither is anyone who believes in him

Their response was to laugh at my words of warning.There were moments that my self-worth and confidence felt reduced to very low levels. What bothered me the most was that the loudest and crudest critics were the very men I opened my home to when they wanted a meal, a friend to speak with, and a place to relax.

Several days after taking the police test I asked God during one my "doubting Thomas moments," if I was going to score number one on the test. It's not that I expected an answer, it's just one of those things I did from time to time. Anyway, that inner voice began to speak to my soul- "Lean not on your own understanding, lean on me and trust me."

Finally, ninety-days after the day the test was administered the results were posted. I told everyone who cared to listen that I was going to place number one on the list of candidates who passed the test. My undying and uncompromising faith in Christ assured me of this.

When the test scores were posted on the police department bulletin board I could not believe my eyes. I finished number forty-four on the list. Totally humiliated and crushed I ran downstairs into the locker room with a broken heart. My feeling of abandonment and devastation was profound.

It didn't take long for my persecutors to start their chorus once again They won! They were now getting rid of the Jesus freak! "What happened to your God?" they yelled. "Your God is so faithful he made sure you came out-what number one the list-oh yeah, number 44, haha!"

The persecution was so intense I was driven to my knees when I returned home from work each night. Jesus, I would ask, "What happened? I trusted you. What happened?" Suddenly, in my deepest depths of despair a warm breeze surrounded me and once again the Holy Spirit spoke to my inner being, "Fear not for I am with you."

At first I thought I was going nuts. But as the moments passed I became convinced that God was going to move a mountain for me

The day after this "encounter with God" I went back to work with a smile on my face. Every time someone messed with me I told them to wait and watch what God was about to do Their replies to me were vulgar, nasty, and yes they thought I cracked up.

Seven days had passed since God spoke to my heart. I awakened at 7.00am and after making some coffee, I picked up the daily newspaper. As I scanned the paper I discovered an article which interested me immediately.

The article reported that the New Jersey Legislature passed a law giving residents of communities where police examinations were held priority on the hiring lists. Another words, if you lived within the community you took the test for your name would be bumped up the list, provided you passed the test.

Guess what? When I checked the revised hiring list I found that the candidates who placed number one to number forty-three lived outside of the Township of Nutley.

I was immediately bumped up to the number one position and within two weeks got hired. The rest is history.

Chapter 9

ANOTHER MOUNTAIN MOVED

Now a veteran police officer with fourteen years of law enforcement experience under my belt I was ready to take another police examination-this one was to become a Sergeant.

Once again I would have to take a civil service promotional examination, just like the one I took when I became a patrolman. And once again, the police department was going to promote one person-the person who scored highest on the examination.

One thing that was different was the number of people taking the test. Instead of hundreds of officers competing for the only sergeants position open, there were only nine of us taking the test. We were all veterans of police work and all very qualified to hold a supervisory position. The competition would be tough.

A few years back I took a sergeants test and failed it. I didn't study and I didn't pray. Hence, through that experience I learned that there is much to be said about the Biblical truth-"faith without works is dead."

This time around I studied hard and prayed daily. I also reminded God of what he did for me many years ago when I prayed the 75th Psalm night and day.

Interestingly, there was very little joking and practically no persecution this time. Many of my peers gained to respect my convictions and others secretly held the belief that I had a "connection" in heaven and they didn't want to get on the wrong side of "Him."

In September of 1991, the police sergeants' examination was administered by the New Jersey Department of Civil Service

When all nine of us completed the test we compared notes and varied in our predicated outcome I didn't express my feeling that I had done well but I was confident that I outscored all my competition. My opinion on how I did when I was asked was simply, "I think I did well "

Several weeks after the examination date the test scores were posted. When I looked at the results I felt disappointed, but not as badly as when I first reacted to the patrolmans exam several years earlier. My score placed me number three on the sergeants promotional list I was not going to get promoted.

After looking over the examination results I approached the officer who outscored all of us and congratulated him. I then went to my car and drove home.

As I was pondering what could have gone wrong, I felt a very warm breeze envelope me. Then, without any warning that very familiar voice started to speak to my spirit, "Ye of little faith . . . "

"What on earth was this all about?" I asked myself. "What is God trying to tell me? I didn't make it this time so that was that," I thought

Several days had passed and everyone in the police department was now talking of other things since the news of the exam results become old.

On the morning of November 7th, I was sitting with the Deputy Chief of Police speaking about a number of police matters when the Mayor's secretary walked into his office. She handed him a piece of paper which contained the official test scores of the sergeants examination we took in September.

As he was looking over the list he expressed his sympathy for me and encouraged me to try again.

Suddenly, he asked, "how long have you been on this police department?" I told him, "fourteen years." He looked at me again and opened his desk draw where he took out a set of sergeant stripes. I told him I didn't think this topic was something to joke about. He replied that he didn't think it was something to joke about either. He then showed me that my seniority score on the final test results was miscalculated and a reworking of the correct figures placed me number one on the promotion list. I became a police sergeant within a short period of time and God once again reminded me through his unique way that mountains could be moved by trusting Him.

Chapter 10
A FAITHFUL PERSON

On January 7, 1997, I received a letter from a police officer who lives in Michigan. He shared with me that he read the "Police Officers Prayer Partner" I had recently published. After giving it to another officer on his department he learned that just about every cop in his precinct wanted a copy of the small booklet. Hence, he requested 500 copies from me.

This was my opportunity to reach dozens of law enforcement officers with the healing words of Christ But no sooner than that thought surfaced I got depressed. I had run out of books, giving most away to financially strapped police officers. I did not have the money to order a new supply. "What was I to do?" I thought.

After pondering this dilemma, I took this matter to the Lord and shared from my heart the need for God to give me the tools to preform the work he called me to do

God always provided the necessities I needed to reach hundreds of men and women in the police profession with the Gospel of Jesus Christ. But this time it looked as if the "well" went dry.

While pouring my heart out to God the words "Trust me, trust me, trust me," kept ringing in my mind So I decided to surrender my will to God and trust Him!

The next day I called a printer and asked him to print 500 copies of the "Police Officers Prayer Partner " I then waited for God to act. It didn't take long Seven days after I put my faith to work I received a letter in the mail with a check attached to it. The letter was from a woman who read my first book, Cops & God "A Loyal Partnership." She explained that her life was so moved by the book that she prayed in thanks to God for what he had done to bless her. While in prayer she felt the presence of the Holy Spirit and was moved to send me a check to do "whatever God led me to do with it " The amount she sent was exactly what I needed to pay for the five-hundred copies of the Prayer Partners I ordered to be printed.I knew immediately what God wanted me to do with the money.

Chapter 11
EVIL TURNED TO GOOD

Since my promotion to Sergeant my responsibilities as a police officer increased dramatically when I was assigned to supervise the community policing unit. This responsibility meant that I would be in a high-visibility position where on a daily basis I was dealing with the people, the politicians, and the press.

Unfortunately, there were a number of people in the community who made a living out of complaining about how our police department was being operated. Every week they would be in city hall criticizing everything the police administration was doing.

It was obvious to numerous people throughout the community that those complaining the loudest were political allies of individuals opposed to the policies which our Police Chief established insofar as the day to day operations of the police department was concerned. Since I was a close friend of the chief and a strong supporter of his administration I had become a target of individuals whose motives to denigrate the police department were political in nature.

On March 20, 1997, I was driving my patrol car on one of our community's main thoroughfares. As I approached an intersection I noticed a friend of mine going into a diner. So I decided to park my police car and have a cup of coffee with her.

Several minutes later, as I was sipping on my coffee, the police dispatcher called and advised me that a citizen called the police desk complaining about my police vehicle being illegally parked. When I asked the dispatcher who the complaintant was I recognized the name to be that of a very vocal political opponent of the police chief. After terminating the call with the dispatcher I went to my police car and found that I backed into a parking space which had a sign displaying, "No Parking Here to Corner." Although I did not see the sign, I realized I was wrong.

As I looked at the sign and my car I realized that if "John Q Public" parked there he would get a summons. In addition, I thought about all the times I spoke with school children about doing the right thing and telling them "when you are caught doing something wrong not to find an easy way out of trouble, but to admit the wrong and move on with life." Here I was challenged with the very words I spoke.

I concluded that this person would call the press and attend a town hall meeting to denigrate me, the chief, and the police department

It didn't take long for me to decide what action to take. Within minutes I took out my summons book and wrote myself a parking ticket. My integrity was too valuable to me to do the simple thing and move the police car I was wrong in parking at that location and I should pay the price like anyone else would have to.

After I issued the summons I immediately drove to the court and paid the seventeen-dollar fine. Believing this was the end of the issue I went to my office

Unbeknown to me a local news reporter learned that I had issued myself a ticket. He immediately contacted the Associated Press and they in turn put the story over the national wire news services What was meant to be a simple act of honesty became an international news story on police integrity

Within two hours every major news outlet from television, radio, and print, converged on our community to meet and interview the "most honest cop in America."

The story spread like wild fire resulting in calls and letters coming into our police department from all over America. The image of the police department was so positive our police agency became known across the country.

Several days later I was told by a friend that the person who called the dispatcher was on a mission to hurt the image of the police department. When he saw the news of what he had sparked he became very upset and angry. His evil motives failed miserably.

What one man meant for evil God turned it into good.

Chapter 12

SHAWN

As told to Steven Rogers by NYPD Officer Stephen Ray

B eing a New York City police officer is rewarding. I love the job and to be frank, I never fully realized the importance of my role in peace keeping until I started reading the Bible and stumbled along the pages which explained how and why a person should accept Jesus Christ as his or her personal Savior.

I think it's really sad to see cops and their family members running in circles trying to save their marriages, homes, jobs, and every other thing they cherish by using drugs, alcohol, gambling, and other destructive things. I guess they are blind like I use to be. But the Bible straightened me out. I'm no Jesus freak. But I am a man who now knows who Jesus is

Last year the NYPD brass decided to review my work and were impressed. They offered to send me to criminal investigation school on the west coast.My supervisor told me that after I completed the courses I would be promoted to detective.

Several weeks after I accepted their offer I was off to San Diego, California, to attend a school on forensic sciences and criminal investigation.

When I arrived at the school it appeared to be a big campus in the middle of nowhere. I met several police officers from throughout the United States and exchanged numerous police stories with them.

During our "Welcome to our School" meeting, all of us were told to pair up with another officer and he would be our partner and roommate for the two weeks we would be there.

Everyone was paired with someone. The number of officers in attendance totaled 76 but one of them did not show up. I learned later that he had an unexpected delay and would be at the school two days later. Hence, I was told that I would not have a roommate or partner for the next two days.

After a number of brief introductions by the instructors I went to my assigned room and unpacked my clothes Since the beds were "bunk beds" I decided to take the top bunk where I lied down and fell asleep.

About an hour later a school staff officer knocked on my door. When I answered it, he told me that the Superintendent wanted to see me. "Already in trouble," I thought.

When I arrived at the "Super's" office he told me he received word from a local police department that a policeman's home was destroyed in a fire and he was at the airport waiting for a flight to New York City to spend a few days with relatives to work out numerous financial matters. While waiting for his flight he learned the jet that he was scheduled to fly on had mechanical problems and the flight was subsequently canceled. Therefore, he needed a place to stay overnight. The nearest hotel with a vacancy was three hours away. Since the school was only one hour from the airport he called and wanted to know if he could occupy a room until morning.

The Superintendent was about to tell the officer that all of the rooms were taken. Then he remembered that I was alone. So he asked me if I wouldn't mind taking in this officer; I told him I wouldn't mind at all.

The superintendent advised me that the officer would be arriving in about an hour.

When I returned to my room I prepared it for my visitor and occupied my bunk again. While in my bed I was reading this book, Cops & God. About a half-hour later one of the cops I met earlier called and invited me to go out to a restaurant. I jumped down from my bunk with the book in my hand and as I was leaving the room I threw the book onto the bottom bunk

While I was out with the other officers, Police Officer Shawn Maxwell, the local officer who lost his home, arrived at the school and was escorted to my room. He unpacked his bags and settled into the bottom bunk.

Two hours later I returned to the room. When I opened the door Officer Maxwell was reading Cops & God. He immediately put the book down and introduced himself.

After some small talk he began to ask me a million questions about the book. He said it moved his soul and he felt encouraged to learn that there were cops who were not ashamed to speak about their faith.

For three hours we talked about life, death, problem solving, the Bible, and Jesus Christ. Shawn told me he had a lot of problems and pressures to deal with and was at his wit's end. While at the airport he had a lot to think about and in desperation called out to God for help. I realized as he was talking that he was a broken hearted man and in the depths of despair.

With a very sincere heart Shawn told me he was a defeated man because he had always tried to do things the fastest and easiest way. He lived life in the fast lane-money, wine, and women, was his life style. These vices lead him to financial trouble, family problems, and eventually to alcoholism.

I told him he had no chance of survival unless he believed Jesus at his word and accepted him as his personal Savior. I recited Bible passages with profound promises and told him about heroes like King David, Moses, and Jesus.

At midnight Shawn Maxwell accepted Jesus Christ as his personal Savior. He was a new man in Christ, forgiven of sin, and now walking in the light of Jesus.After saying a prayer of thanks, we went to sleep.

The next morning I awakened at 6˙00am and noticed the room was empty. "Where was Shawn?" I thought.

As I looked around I noticed a note pinned up on the entrance door with a baseball cap next to it. I jumped off my bed and removed both items.

"Dear Stephen, I was awakened last night by an officer who told me that I got a message that a flight was rescheduled to NYC for 3:00am.If I wanted to catch it, I had to pack my bags and leave soon. I didn't wake you because I knew you were tired. Thank you for taking the time to share with me the greatest story I was ever told. I am now part of God's army and I feel good about it. Thanks for showing me the way to Christ. God Bless you. "

After I finished reading the note I picked up the baseball cap and tried it on As I looked in the mirror I noticed the words written on its front - "City of Angels."

As a chill ran up and down my spin I wondered if Shawn Maxwell was really an . . . end.

POLICE OFFICERS
PRAYER PARTNER

Very few people in the law enforcement profession know that the Bible speaks about police
officers.

Biblical history records that the first police officer to
have an encounter with God and to accept Jesus Christ
as his personal savior was a Roman precinct commander
named Cornelius.

Cornelius was in command of the Roman Police Headquarters in the city of Caesarea in Palestine. He was
known to be an honest cop and devoted to his family and
God.

The important biblical event regarding Cornelius is that
he was the first Gentile to convert to Christianity after
hearing the apostle Peter preaching in the streets near the
police station.

We read in the book of Matthew, Chapter 8, of another
"police-God" encounter. Matthew recorded an astonish-
ing confession of faith by a policeman who asked Jesus
to heal his ill and suffering servant. When Jesus told this
bold cop he would heal his servant the police officer
replied, "Lord, I do not deserve to have you come under
my roof, but just say the word and my servant will be
healed. For I myself am a man under authority with

officers under me. I tell this one to go and he goes, that one to come, and he comes " When Jesus heard this cop's confession of faith he said, "I have not found anyone in Israel with such great faith . . " The servant was healed at that very hour.

One of the most profound biblical events involving police officers and God took place at the Crucifixion of Jesus Christ. It was at Golgotha where a police officer publicly admitted that Jesus was the Son of God.

As he was dying on the cross, Jesus began to call his father. Immediately one of the officers present ran and

got a sponge, filled it with vinegar, put it on a stick, and offered Jesus to drink it. When Jesus refused another officer ordered everyone to leave him alone. At that moment the earth shook and a third police officer proclaimed what is now remembered by all generations since that time-"Truly this man is the Son of God."

Police officers have always been by the side of Jesus Christ from the time he began his ministry to the day he went home to be with his father in Heaven.

May history record that police officers in the 21st Century walk as close to God as their brothers did in early biblical times. *-Steven L. Rogers*

Romans 13.4

L et every soul be subject unto the higher powers, for there is no power but of God: the powers be are ordained of God. Whoever resists the power resists the ordinance of God: and they that resist shall receive to themselves damnation. For police officers are not a terror to law abiding citizens, but to criminals. Obey the law, for police officers are agents of God who enforce the law . . . the police officer carries his weapon not in vain . . He is an agent of God called to enforce the laws of man and of God by bringing to justice those who commit criminal evil acts.

THE POLICE OFFICER AND ANGER, ANXIETY

Promotional examinations, making critical decisions, changes in assignments, rumors, and anger over the crimes you witness can bring a great toll upon your life. When things seem to be so overwhelming take a moment and read what God's word says about these things.

Be anxious for nothing, but in everything by prayer and supplication with thanksgiving let your troubles and problems be made known to God. By doing this, the peace of God shall keep your mind and heart focused on Jesus Christ. Philippians 4.6-9

When you become angry do not sin. Do not let the day

end in anger. Make peace with everyone who wrongs you either by speaking with them or praying for them. Ephesians 4.26

Be quick to listen, slow to speak, and slow to anger, for your anger will not please God. James 1.19-20

The Bible declares that there is nothing wrong with a person who becomes angry. There is something called a righteous anger. However, God does not want us to sin when we become angry. Therefore, it is important to keep our cool, take a deep breath before we act, and remember the words written in this "Prayer Partner."

THE POLICE OFFICER AND BLESSINGS

Police officers are peacemakers. The job of a police officer is to maintain law and order in a society becoming more chaotic as each day passes. People have the police to call when they are in need. God blesses his police officers for keeping the peace.

Blessed are the peacemakers for they shall be called the children of God. Matthew 5.9

To the counselors of peace is joy. Proverbs 12.20

Blessed is the man that walks not in the counsel of the ungodly, nor stands in the way of the sinner, nor sits in the seat of the scornful. His delight is in the law of the Lord: and in his law does he meditate day and night. And he shall be like a tree planted by the rivers of water and whatever he does shall prosper. Psalm 1

God is telling us that if we do not walk, stand, or sit, with people who seek to commit evil acts, we will be blessed. Sadly, many police officers choose to live in the fast lane and end up with the counsel of the ungodly and their lives become a mess. The officers who walk with God are the officers who will reap answered prayer and blessings from above.

THE POLICE OFFICER AND CARE, COMFORT

Police personnel are called upon to care for all different kinds of people in a very troubled society. Who then shall police officers call upon when they encounter their own personal problems? They can count on Jesus Christ!

God will meet all your needs. Philippians 4.19

Behold, God is my helper. Psalm 54.5

The Lord will guide you in times of trouble. Isaiah 58 11

Thy rod and thy staff shall comfort me. Psalm 23.4

THE POLICE OFFICER AND DEBT, DEPRESSION, DISAPPOINTMENT

Police officers suffer from many problems as a result of disappointment, depression, and debt. Many cops try to escape from their problems by drinking alcohol, taking drugs, or in unfortunate cases committing suicide. The Bible is a resource every cop can turn to when in need of solutions to any problem he encounters. God's word is known as the "Sword of the Spirit." The Lord goes before you and will be with you; he will never leave you nor forsake you. Do not fear or be disappointed. Deuteronomy 31.8 God is our refuge and strength, an ever present help in time of trouble. Psalm 46.1

THE POLICE OFFICER AND ENCOURAGEMENT

You are a chosen generation, a royal priesthood, a Holy nation, a people belonging to God . . . 1 Peter 2 9

My help comes from God. ...He will not let you stumble or fall. He who watches over you will not slumber. Psalm 121.2,3

He shall cover you with his feathers and under his wings you shall trust: his truth shall be your shield and buckler. Psalm 91.4

THE POLICE OFFICER AND THE FAMILY

The family unit is God's most sacred institution which began when he created the first man and woman, Adam and Eve.

The Book of Genesis reveals that this couple was blessed by God and eventually had two sons, Cain and Abel.

But something very terrible happened to this family. First, the well-known incident in the Garden of Eden took place. Then one of their sons killed his brother. This once very blessed family became divided and fragmented. How could such a thing happen to a family so richly blessed?

Many police families find themselves in similar situations as the first family. For a while they are happy and suddenly their lives are turned upside down bringing to ruin their household.

The Bible reveals to us how this happen- ed to Adam and Eve and how it is happening to police families today.

The family of Adam and Eve was God's finest work. He loved them, protected them, and gave them everything a family would want. All he asked for in return was for them to obey him. " Do not touch the tree of knowledge .. " God commanded. As soon as God left the garden Adam and Eve violated his command after being tempted by Satan. To make matters worse, when God returned and asked them what happened they lied.

God blesses police officers and their families because he loves them. His instruction to the cop is clear- do what is right, worship God, trust God, obey God.

For a while, many police officers follow God's instructions and they reap his blessings. But like the ser- pent in the Garden of Eden, someone comes along and tempts the police officer to commit sins against God. Most of these sins are adultery, pride, alcohol and drug abuse, abuse, corruption, and many other acts which violate a police officer's oath of office. While the cop is committing these violations of God's law, he/ she does not see the destructive path they are on. They are blind! Eventually they end up in the same condition as Adam and Eve.

Romans 6.23 states "the wages of sin is death." When police officers play with the fire of sin, they get burned to death.

Since police officers are God's chosen people to fight the evils of this world, Satan has targeted them as a priority in his mission to destroy God's Kingdom. Once the peacemakers are compromised, the peace in our society is at risk.

Every police officer can protect himself from the

temptation of sin by keeping his/her eyes on Christ. The Book of Matthew, chapter 7.24-27 states that if we keep our eyes on Christ and build our homes on the foundation in which God gives us we will reap his blessings. However, that same area of scripture tells us that those who choose to build their lives on the empty promises of man will see their homes fall. The choice as to how and where each police officer builds his/her home is each individuals to make. The outcome however, is clear. Blessed is the man who walks not in the counsel of the ungodly, nor stands in the way of the sinner, nor sits in the seat of the scornful ... but his delight is in the law of the Lord. Psalm 1.1-2

THE POLICE OFFICER AND FAITH, FELLOWSHIP

Faith cometh by hearing, hearing by the word of God. Romans 10.17

Now faith is the substance of things hoped for, the evidence of things not seen. Hebrews 11.1

Faith without works is dead. James 2.17

God is faithful, by whom we are called unto fellowship with His Son Jesus Christ. 1 John 1.3

Behold, I stand at the door and knock if any man hears my voice and opens the door I will fellowship with him and he with me. Revelation 3.20

THE POLICE OFFICER AND GROWTH, GRIEF, GUILT

Being confident of this very thing, that he who began a good work in you will perform it until it is done. Philippians 1.6

When you pass through troubled waters I will be with you. Isaiah 43.2

God himself will be with you and be your God. He will wipe every tear from your eyes. Revelation 21.3.4

But you are a forgiving God, full of grace and compassion, slow to anger and abounding in love. Neh: 9 17

THE POLICE OFFICER AND HEAVEN, HOLINESS, HELL

Look down from thy Holy habitation, from Heaven, and bless thy people. Deuteronomy 26 15

His divine power has given us all things pertinent to life and godliness, through the knowledge of Him that called us to glory and virtue. 2.Peter 1 3

Throughout the entire Bible hell is identified as an eternal place of torment-reserved for people who sin against God and fail to repent. The only way to escape a sentence to hell is to escape from sin- Repent without delay!

THE POLICE OFFICER AND INSPIRATION, JOY

And there is a spirit in man: and the inspiration of the Almighty giveth them understanding. Job 32.8
God will not forget your work and the love shown him as you help his people. Hebrews 6.10

May the God of hope fill you with joy and peace as you trust in Him. Revelation 15.13

Ask and you will receive. John 16.24

Thou will show me the path of life. In his presence is fullness of joy. Psalm 16.11

THE POLICE OFFICER AND THE KINGDOM OF GOD

Blessed are the poor in spirit for theirs is the Kingdom of Heaven. Matthew 5.3

Jesus said . . Verily, Verily, I say unto thee except a man be born again he cannot see the Kingdom of God. John 3.3

Confirming the souls of the disciples, and exhorting them to continue in the faith, and that we must through much tribulation enter into the Kingdom of God. Acts 14.22

THE POLICE OFFICER AND LOVE, LOYALTY

My love for you will not be shaken. Isaiah 43.1

For God so loved the world that he gave us his only begotten son, that whoever believes in him shall not perish but have everlasting life. John 3.16

He takes great delight in you, he will quiet you with his love, he will rejoice over you with singing. Zephaniah 3.7

I am the bread of life. He who comes to me will never go hungry and he who believes in me will never go thirsty. John 6.35

THE POLICE OFFICER AND MERCY, NEEDS

Do not remember the sins of my youth, nor my transgressions, according to your mercy remember me . . . Psalm 25.7

Blessed are the merciful. Matthew 5.7

I trust in the mercy of God. Psalm 52.8

Let us therefore come boldly to the throne of grace, that we may obtain mercy and find grace to help in time of need. Hebrews 4.16

THE POLICE OFFICER AND OBEDIENCE, PRAYER

Behold, to obey is better than sacrifice. 1 Samuel 15.22

Behold, I set before you today a blessing . . . the blessing if you obey the commandments of the Lord your God. Deuteronomy 11.26

Obey those who bring you the Word of God for they watch out for your soul. Hebrews 13.17

The effectual fervent prayer of a righteous man availeth much. James 5.16

THE POLICE OFFICER AND QUIETNESS, TRUSTING, REDEMPTION, REASONING, SALVATION

Take heed and be quiet; do not fear or be faint hearted. Isaiah 7.4

With Him there is abundant redemption. Psalm 130.7

Come now and let us reason together saith the Lord. Isaiah 1.18

We know this that He is Christ, the Savior. John 4.42

He who trusts in the Lord mercy shall surround him. Psalm 32.10

THE POLICE OFFICER AND UNDERSTANDING GOD, HIS WISDOM, VICTORY

The wisdom of the prudent is to under- stand God. Proverbs 14.8

Because you have asked for understanding to discern justice, I have given you a wise and understanding heart. 1 Kings 3.11

Understanding is a well spring of life. Proverbs 16.22

Thanks be to God who gives victory through our Lord Jesus Christ. 1 Corinthians 15.57

POLICE OFFICERS PRAYER OF SALVATION

Lord God, I confess that I am a sinner and that Jesus came to this earth and shed his blood so that my sins may be forgiven. Lord, I confess that Jesus Christ rose from the dead and now sits at the right hand of the father. I now accept Jesus Christ as my Personal Lord, Savior, and Master. Amen.

If thou shalt confess with thy mouth that Jesus Christ is Lord and shall believe in thy heart that god raised him from the dead, thou shalt be saved. Romans 10 9

GOD BLESS YOU.